MW01257319

CHOSEN

Your Life Is Marked for Distinction

JOEL OSTEEN

NEW YORK • NASHVILLE

Also by Joel Osteen

CHOSEN

Copyright © 2025 by Joel Osteen

Cover design by Faceout Studio, Jeff Miller
Cover copyright © 2025 by Hachette Book Group, Inc.

Hachette Book Group supports the right to free expression and the value of copyright. The purpose of copyright is to encourage writers and artists to produce the creative works that enrich our culture.

The scanning, uploading, and distribution of this book without permission is a theft of the author's intellectual property. If you would like permission to use material from the book (other than for review purposes), please contact permissions@hbgusa.com. Thank you for your support of the author's rights.

FaithWords
Hachette Book Group
1290 Avenue of the Americas, New York, NY 10104
faithwords.com
@FaithWords / @FaithWordsBooks

First Edition: July 2025

FaithWords is a division of Hachette Book Group, Inc. The FaithWords name and logo are registered trademarks of Hachette Book Group, Inc.

The publisher is not responsible for websites (or their content) that are not owned by the publisher.

The Hachette Speakers Bureau provides a wide range of authors for speaking events. To find out more, go to hachettespeakersbureau.com or email HachetteSpeakers@hbgusa.com.

FaithWords books may be purchased in bulk for business, educational, or promotional use. For information, please contact your local bookseller or the Hachette Book Group Special Markets Department at special.markets@hbgusa.com.

Literary development: Lance Wubbels Literary Services, Bloomington, Minnesota.

Library of Congress Cataloging-in-Publication Data

Names: Osteen, Joel author
Title: Chosen : your life is marked for distinction / Joel Osteen.
Description: First edition. | New York : Faith Words, 2025. |
    Identifiers: LCCN 2025002813 | ISBN 9781546008828 |
    ISBN 9781546008835 ebook
Subjects: LCSH: Self-actualization (Psychology)—Religious
    aspects—Christianity | Self-confidence—Religious
    aspects—Christianity | Christian life
Classification: LCC BV4598.2 .O864 2025 | DDC 158.1—dc23/eng/20250404
LC record available at https://lccn.loc.gov/2025002813

ISBN: 9781546008828 (paper over board), 9781546008835 (ebook)

Printed in the United States of America

LSC-C

Printing 1, 2025

Contents

1

You Are Marked for Distinction

When we honor God with our lives and do our best to keep Him first place, the Scripture says He puts favor on your life that causes you to be different. It's a favor that makes a distinction between you and those who don't honor God. The Scripture speaks of how you've been chosen, called out, set apart. Some older translations say you are "a peculiar people." I think a better phrase is "a different people." You're not ordinary; you're not like everyone else. You've been marked with a distinction. Numbers 6 says that

God's face will shine down on you and cause you to stand out.

This distinctive favor causes you to prosper when others are struggling. You recover from a difficulty when others get stuck. You have protection when others face calamity. There's a marked difference. You have an advantage. You're not doing life by yourself, just on your own strength, your talent, your connections. There is a force breathing behind you, guiding you, protecting you, favoring you. The Most High God has set you apart. He could have chosen anyone, but He handpicked you, called you out, and said, "That's one of Mine." Right now, His face is shining down on you. Don't go through life thinking that you're average, that you can never accomplish your dreams. Put your shoulders back. Hold your head high. You're a part of the called-out group.

God has set you up for a distinctively favored life. That means He's chosen you for blessings you didn't work for, for promotion you didn't deserve. The Scripture says, "For houses you didn't build, for vineyards you didn't plant." It's not because of who you are; it's because of whose you are. You've been marked with favor. When you realize this, you'll pray bold prayers. You'll dream big dreams. You'll expect things to happen for you that may not happen for others. When others are afraid and upset and worried, you'll be at peace, knowing that you've been set apart, that there's a hedge around you that the enemy cannot cross, that you have distinctive favor.

A Hedge of Protection

When the Israelites were in slavery, God told Moses to go and tell Pharaoh to let His people go. But Pharaoh wouldn't listen. He kept refusing. God sent plague after plague on Pharaoh and his people. Their water supply was turned to blood. Millions of locusts ate their crops and destroyed their land. What's interesting is that the Israelites, some two million people, lived right next door, but these plagues never affected them. At one point, there were hordes of frogs. Everywhere Pharaoh's people looked there were frogs—in their homes, in their food, in their beds. They were so frustrated. On the Israeli side there were no frogs. Life went on as usual. But Pharaoh still wouldn't change his mind.

When God was about to send swarms of flies into the Egyptian houses, He said to Pharaoh, "I will deal differently with the land where My people live. No swarms of flies will be there. I will make a distinction between you and My people." Millions and millions of flies came into Pharaoh's palace and all the houses of the Egyptians. The flies were so dense the people couldn't see, couldn't eat, couldn't sleep. Their land was ruined by flies. But right next door, the Israelites had no flies. I can hear the Israelites saying to their neighbors, "I'll let you borrow my fly swatter. We don't need it over here." It didn't make sense in the natural. This was the hand of God putting a distinction on His chosen people.

God has put that same distinction on you. When He breathed life into you, He marked you for favor, marked you for blessing, marked you to stand out. What will defeat others won't be able to defeat you. This is why you don't have to live worried—worried about your safety, worried about your future, worried about your children—even though there are so many negative things in the world, so much crime and violence. It may be happening all around you, but you have an advantage. God has put a distinction on you. The psalmist said, "A thousand may fall at my side, ten thousand at my right hand, but it will not come near me." God has placed a hedge of protection around you and your family. For the enemy to get to you, he has to ask God for permission.

I'm not saying negative things will never happen. That's not reality. I'm saying you are protected by the One who controls it all. If God allows it to happen, He's promised that He will turn it somehow and use it for your good.

Marked for Distinction

Pharaoh still wouldn't let the Israelites go after the plague of flies. Then Moses told him, "There's about to be a plague on all your livestock, your horses, camels, goats, and sheep." But once again, the Scripture says God put a distinction on the livestock of the Israelites so that not one of the Israelites' animals would die. Notice a distinction is even on your property—your house, your car, your belongings. The next day, just as God had said, all their oppressors' livestock died, but not one animal belonging to the Israelites.

I'm sure some of Pharaoh's people thought, *That's it. I'm going to the Israeli side. These frogs, flies, and locusts are making my life miserable.* They moved over to the Israelites' land, set up temporary homes...but everywhere they went, the plagues followed them. It wasn't where the Israelites were that kept them from the plagues. It was what was on them—the distinction, the favor, the blessing that comes from being a child of the Most High God.

You and I have that same blessing. We may have things around us that could harm us, keep us from our dreams, bring us down. Stay in faith. There is a distinction on your life, on your property, on your children, on your career, and on your health that is put there by the Creator of the universe.

When I was growing up, a friend of ours was a successful businessman who owned hundreds of acres of orange groves. One winter day, it was predicted that there was going to be a hard freeze, which was unusual in that part of the country. It almost never froze there. He knew the freeze would destroy all his crops and cost him thousands of dollars. In the natural, there was nothing he could do. That's what all the circumstances said. But he understood this principle that God had put a distinction on his property, that God had a hedge around his business. Instead of being defeated, thinking, *Oh, great! Bad luck this year,* he went out and walked all around his orange groves, thanking God that his trees would live, thanking Him that they wouldn't freeze and that he would have a harvest that year. When the other farmers who lived around him heard what he did, that he prayed for his trees, they thought he was so strange, so far out. They made fun and ridiculed him.

The next day the big freeze came in and lasted a little over twenty-four hours. The other farmers were very discouraged, trying to figure out how they were going to make a living, not having a harvest that year. But a couple weeks later, there was the most unusual sight. Our friend's property, hundreds and hundreds of acres, had the most beautiful, healthy orange trees. The trees on the properties next to his, on all four sides, were totally dead. It was as though somebody had put a blanket over our friend's property. The other farmers were so amazed that instead of making fun of him, they asked him, "Next time will you pray for our crops as well?"

I know some people will think, *Joel, that's just a lucky break. That's just the way the clouds must have formed that day, just the way the winds must have blown.* No, that was the hand of God putting a distinction on his property. That was God's face shining down on him. God has put this same distinction on you. Don't talk yourself out of it. "Well, business is slow. A couple of my coworkers got laid off. I don't see how I can get out of debt." Your job is not your source. God is your source. The economy doesn't determine whether or not you're blessed; God does. He has already chosen and marked you for favor. He's already put this distinction on your life. Dare to pray bold prayers. Believe for unusual favor. Take the limits off God. You've been set apart.

A Supply Line That Never Runs Dry

A lady told me how she was having her best year in her career. She works in a sales position, and her whole industry in general was down. They were going through a transition. Her coworkers were struggling, and her competitors were way down. But she said, "It seems as though every time I turn around, a new account is finding me." She told how on three or four occasions she was at the right place at the right time. Unexpectedly, business dropped into her lap. She made the statement, "Joel, I'm supposed to go out and find new customers, but it's as if new customers are always finding me." Psalm 37 says, "Even in famine, the righteous will have more than enough." Even in a downtime, because she's the righteous, because she has this distinction of being chosen by God, she's seeing increase and favor.

Here's the key: As long as you stay close to God, as long as you keep Him first place, you are connected to a supply line that will never run dry. Even in a slow economy, God will cause clients to find you. Even when the medical report says no way, you are connected to a supply line filled with health, wholeness, and restoration.

When you don't see how you can accomplish your dreams, don't get discouraged. You have a supply line connected with good breaks, the right people, ideas, and creativity.

I have friends who live in another state. They were trying to sell their home, but the housing market in their area was very depressed. A large company nearby had gone out of business, and that's where many of their neighbors worked. Now there was a surplus of homes on the market. On their street alone, there were twelve houses for sale. The average time for a house to sell back then was a year and a half. Their realtor had already told them, "Don't be in a hurry. This is going to be a long, drawn-out process, and the value could go down and down." In the natural, it didn't look good. But instead of expecting the worst, thinking their house would never sell, this young couple was bold enough to believe that God had put a distinction on their property like He did for the Israelites. Every morning they said, "Father, thank You that You're causing our house to stand out. Thank You that people are being drawn to it." Six weeks after they put the house on the market, they received a contract and sold it. At the closing, they were talking to the new owners, who said they had looked at many different properties, even houses that were a better value and in a better location. But they said, "When we came to your house, there was just something different about it. We felt a peace. We knew it was supposed to be ours."

What is that? Distinctive favor, where God causes it to stand out. I wonder what would happen if you would get up every morning and say, "Father, thank You that Your face is shining down on me. Thank You that You put a distinction on my life." All the circumstances may say otherwise. "You'll never get well. You'll never meet the right person. Your house is never going to sell." Don't believe those lies. You have to have a boldness like this young couple to believe that there's something different about you, that you have a right to be blessed, you have a right to see favor. I don't mean arrogantly, but in humility, knowing that because of who you are, a child of the Most High, He has chosen and set you apart, He's put favor on you that causes you to stand out. Like the Israelites, God has put a distinction on your life, on your property, on your career. You have an advantage. If you get this down in your spirit, you'll start praying these bold prayers and believing for things that seem impossible.

Keep Rising to the Top

This is what my father did. He tried for many years to build a new church sanctuary, but every time he tried to move forward, he felt an unrest, knowing it wasn't the right time. In 1986, Houston was in one of the deepest recessions our city had ever seen. Businesses were going bankrupt. People were struggling. My father had just been released from the hospital after having open-heart surgery. It was a few weeks before Christmas. It seemed like the worst time to start any project, especially the worst time to try to raise funds. Deep down he could hear God telling him to do it right then. But he thought, *God, that doesn't make sense. This is a downtime. People aren't going to have extra income. How can we possibly raise these funds?* He heard God whisper, "Son, I want you to do it now so people will know it's Me and not anybody else."

God likes to do unusual things in your life so others will be drawn to Him. A year and a half later, they dedicated a new six-million-dollar auditorium totally debt free. Even in a down economy, even when critics said no way and circumstances said it's not going to happen, God said, "Don't worry. It may be that way in the natural, but I'm a supernatural God. I put a distinction on you that will cause you to defy the odds, to have more than enough even in famine."

In the Scripture, Joseph went through a lot of bad breaks. He was betrayed by his brothers, sold into slavery, put in prison for something he didn't do. For thirteen years, you could say, he was in

a famine. He could have been bitter and negative. "God, why did You let this happen to me?"
But Joseph understood this principle. Despite
the opposition, he kept being his best. No matter how much people tried to push him down,
he kept rising to the top. He worked for a man
by the name of Potiphar. Joseph was so excellent
in what he did, he had such a good attitude, that
Potiphar put him in charge of his household. The
Scripture says that Potiphar noticed the Lord was
with Joseph, giving him success in everything he
did. Potiphar saw the distinction.

God wants to bless you in such a way that
people notice. He wants to show out in your life
to where people say, "You mean you sold your
house in six weeks when it should have taken a
year and a half? You mean all the orange groves
froze, but yours didn't? You mean you built the
sanctuary in the middle of a recession? Joel, you
mean your mother had terminal cancer in 1981,
but she's still alive today? You mean you're having
church in the former Compaq Center?"

That's what distinctive favor does. It causes you to stand out. You may have seen some of this in the past, but you need to get ready. You haven't seen anything yet. God is about to do some things in your life that are going to get you noticed. People are going to see it wasn't just your talent, your ability, your connections. It was the hand of God opening doors that no man can open, taking you where you could not go on your own.

The Scripture says God began to bless Potiphar for Joseph's sake. Because of the distinction on Joseph's life, people around him began to get blessed. Your company should be glad to have you at work. When you get there, the blessing gets there. When you show up, favor shows up. Some of your friends, relatives, and coworkers don't even know they're being blessed because of you.

What's interesting is that Joseph was a slave. He didn't have a prestigious position. He was taking care of the household, doing repairs, mowing, cleaning. On the other hand, Potiphar was one of the highest-ranking military officials of that day. People looked up to him, saluted him, and did whatever he commanded. You would think that Joseph would be blessed for Potiphar's sake. It was just the opposite.

What am I saying? The distinction God put on you is more powerful than positions, than titles, than education. When God's face is shining down on you, you'll not only rise higher, but it's so powerful that even the people around you will begin to get blessed.

I know a man who used to do some consulting work with us years ago. We were a small client compared to most of his clients. He consulted for the big Fortune 500 companies and had a really impressive résumé. We got to know each other and went out to lunch a couple times. After about a year, he said, "Joel, ever since I started working for your ministry, my business has gone to a new level." He named client after client that he had picked up—big, impressive names. He turned to the associate standing next to us and said, "I like working for Joel. He brings me good luck." He called it "luck," but I know it's the distinction God puts on our life. It's the favor He's placed on you and me.

Your Location Doesn't Determine the Blessing

In the Scripture, when Abraham moved to a new country with his family, his nephew Lot, and all his flocks and herds, he found a beautiful piece of land, with luscious green pastures and peaceful ponds. It looked like a postcard. But after a few months, he realized the land couldn't sustain all the flocks and herds. He told Lot to choose where he wanted to live with his flocks and herds, and Abraham would take his and go elsewhere. Lot said he wanted to stay right there, in the best part of the land. Instead of arguing, Abraham took the high road and moved to a different part of the country. But this time, all he could find was land that was dry and barren. Instead of lush, beautiful green pastures, it was more like the desert, with rocks and sand and very little water.

In the natural, Abraham should have struggled. He should have seen his crops dry up and his business go down to nothing. But it was just the opposite. Hardly any time passed before his flocks and herds multiplied so much and that dry barren land had turned into a beautiful oasis. In fact, the Scripture speaks of how he had so much that he became one of the wealthiest men of that time.

As with Abraham, even if you're in the desert, because of the distinction God put on you, you're still going to flourish. Your location doesn't determine the blessing. What God put on you determines the blessing. When He chose and called you out, He marked you for favor. Wherever you go, the blessing goes. You might not have the perfect job, people might not be treating you right, and you might not be getting the credit you deserve. That's okay, because you're not working unto people, you're working unto

God. People don't determine your destiny; God does. Keep being your best, honoring God, and as with Joseph, God will cause you to be noticed. He'll cause you to stand out. Potiphar will come looking for you. At the right time, God will either turn that around by promoting you, or He'll move you somewhere else.

But the key is to not think that you can wait until you're out of the desert and then you're going to have a good attitude, then you're going to start being your best. There's something on you right now that will cause you to prosper in the middle of the desert. Lot wasn't making good decisions. He wasn't honoring God. He was blessed as long as Abraham was there, but when Abraham left, the blessing left. Lot's fields dried up. His flocks went down to nothing. He ended up leaving that place. Eventually, Abraham had to go and rescue him and his family.

As with Lot, there are people whom God put into your life right now who are being blessed because of you. They may never realize it. They may never tell you thank you. Don't worry, because God is keeping the records. Those are seeds that you're sowing. He'll make sure you are blessed in a greater way. Back then, they would even pray to the God of Abraham. When they saw how blessed Abraham was, how he flourished even in the desert, they thought, *If we can get to his God, maybe we'll be blessed.* God wants to put such a distinction on you. He wants you to stand out in such a way that people want what you have. They'll say, "I'm going to pray to the God of those people at Lakewood. I'm going to pray to the God of Robert, to the God of Susan, to the God of Maria. Look at how blessed she is, so faithful, so generous, so talented. If I can get to her God, I believe I can be blessed."

This Favor Accelerates Your Dreams

I received an email from a lady named Ruby. One night after dinner, she and her husband,

George, took the leftovers out of their refrigerator and were playing with different recipes to make gumbo. They were trying different combinations, different spices, just having fun, seeing what they could create. They came up with a recipe they liked so much that they started selling it door to door. It was a big hit. Everyone loved their gumbo. One night they saw a television commercial about a large grocery store chain that was looking for contestants for a cooking competition. Whoever won would get to put their product on these stores' shelves. They sent their gumbo in, and out of six hundred submissions, they were notified that they made it into the top twenty-five. They were so excited. They kept praying and believing.

A few months later the grand prize winner was announced, but unfortunately it wasn't them. It was as if the wind had been taken out of their sails. They attend Lakewood, and I'd just spoken about how God strategically orchestrates our steps, how He doesn't always take us in sequence from A to B to C. Sometimes He'll take you two steps ahead, one step back, and then five steps forward. The key is to trust Him in those times when it feels like you're going in the wrong direction.

Several months later, Ruby was in our Wednesday night service when she received a phone call from her contact at that grocery store chain. She went out into the lobby and answered it. They said, "Even though you didn't win, we like your gumbo so much that we still want to put it on our shelves." She and George were thrilled. They couldn't believe it.

But part of this distinction is that God wants to accelerate your dreams coming to pass. He's going to speed things up, make it happen faster than you thought. After the store chain had carried the gumbo for a short time, they called again and said, "Your gumbo is so great that we want you to create a whole food line for us, and we'll help you get it started." In less than a year, this couple went from one night of playing in their kitchen with leftovers to having the availability to create a food line in one of the largest grocery store chains around.

God knows how to get you noticed. His face is shining down on you right now. He's put a distinction on your life, your property, your career, your children. It's going to cause you to stand out. It's going to open doors that you could never open. It's going to bring opportunity, the right people, and good breaks. You're not doing life alone. You have the most powerful force in the universe breathing in your direction right now. You've been called out, set apart, chosen to live a distinctively favored life. Now do your part. Pray bold prayers. Take the limits off God. Believe for your dreams. If you do this, God is going to show out in your life in amazing ways. As with Abraham, you will prosper in a desert. As with Joseph, He's going to cause you to be noticed. And as with Ruby and George, it's going to happen faster than you think.

2

You Are Chosen

There is an underlying pressure in our society to be number one. If we're not the best, the leader, the fastest, the most talented, the most beautiful, or the most successful, we're taught to not feel good about ourselves. We have to work harder. We have to run faster. We must stay ahead.

If a neighbor moves into a new house, instead of being inspired and happy for them, we're intimidated into thinking, *That's making me look bad. I've got to keep up.* If a coworker gets a promotion, we feel as though we're falling behind. We know we don't measure up when a friend tells us they're going to Europe on vacation, and we're going to our grandmother's twelve miles down the road.

If we're not careful, there will always be someone or something making us feel we're not up to par. We're not far enough along. As long as you compare your situation to others, you will never feel good about yourself, because there will always be somebody more talented, more beautiful, more successful.

You have to realize you're not running their race. You're running your race. You have a specific calling and assignment. God has given you exactly what you need for the race that's been designed for you. A friend, a coworker, or a relative may seem to have a more significant gift. They can outrun you and outperform you. That's okay. You're not competing with them. They have what they need for their assignment. You have what you need for your assignment.

Don't make the mistake of trying to keep up

with them, wondering, *Why can't I sing like that?*
Why can't I be the manager? When am I going to
reach their level? If you're not content with your
gift, comfortable with who God made you to
be, you'll go through life frustrated and envious,
thinking, *I wish I had her looks. I wish I had his*
talent. I wish I owned their business. No, if you had
what they have, it wouldn't help you; it would
hinder you. They have a different assignment.

Quit trying to outperform others, and then
you'll start to feel good about yourself. Don't
condition your contentment upon moving into
a new neighborhood, having your business catch
up to someone else's, or getting a promotion. One
of the best things I've ever learned is to be comfortable with who God made me to be. I don't
have to outperform anyone to feel good about
myself. I don't have to outbuild, outdrive, out-
race, outminister, or outproduce anyone. It's not
about anyone else. It's about becoming who God
made me to be.

Accept the Gift God Has Given You

As a young man, God said to Jeremiah, "Before I formed you in your mother's womb I chose you. Before you were born I set you apart. I called you to speak to the nations." What He said to Jeremiah, He says to each of us. Before you were born, the Most High God not only knew you but He chose you. He handpicked you and put a calling on your life. He put greatness in you and gave you a purpose. He's destined you to leave your mark. But it's easy to acquiesce as Jeremiah did and say, "I can't do that. I'm too young. I don't have the boldness. Why would they listen to me?" We can all make excuses, but God is saying, "Stop saying that."

You have to accept the gift that God has given you. You shouldn't feel less-than if someone seems to have a more significant gift. It takes a secure person to say, "I'm comfortable with who I am." I hear ministers who have deep voices and are great orators. They can move the congregation with their words and give you chill bumps, and I stand up in front of my congregation with my Texas twang. This is what I've been given. I can improve it. I can develop it. I can cultivate it, but my voice is never going to sound like I'm James Earl Jones. There is always going to be somebody who can minister better, who is further along and more experienced. But you know what? That doesn't bother me. I know God chose me. I know I have the gifts I need for my assignment.

Here's the key: You don't have to have a great gift for God to use it in a great way. Do you know what David's gift was that put him on the throne? It wasn't his leadership skills. It wasn't his dynamic personality. It wasn't his ability to write and play music. It was his gift to sling a rock. He was a sharpshooter with a sling. He could have thought, *Oh, great. Big deal. I'm good with a sling. This is not going to get me anywhere. I'm out in the shepherds' fields, alone, no people. Just a bunch of sheep.* But it was his ability with a sling, that seemingly insignificant gift, that enabled him to defeat Goliath and eventually put David on the throne.

Quit discounting your calling and the gift that God has given you. It may seem insignificant. "I'm not as smart as my sister. Not as talented as my coworker. Can't write the software like my colleague." Maybe not, but there's something God has given you that's unique, something that will propel you into your destiny, something that will cause you to leave your mark on this generation. Don't believe the lies that say, "You're average. There's nothing special about you. You don't have the personality that your cousin has. You don't have the talent of your friend." No, but you have a sling. It's not so much what you have. It's the anointing that God puts on it. Your gift may seem ordinary, but when God breathes on it, you'll defeat a giant twice your size. You'll be promoted beyond your talent. You'll go places where you weren't qualified. You didn't have the experience. You weren't next in line, but suddenly a door opened. Suddenly you defeated the giant. Suddenly the dream comes to pass.

Don't Wait for a Title or Position

Too often we pursue titles and positions, thinking we'll feel good about ourselves when we have them. "When I make it to sales manager, when I get on the varsity cheerleading squad, when I'm the head usher, the senior partner, the lead supervisor..." That's fine. There's nothing wrong with titles, but you don't need a title to do what God has called you to do. Don't wait for people to approve you, affirm you, or validate you. Use your gift, and the title will come.

If David had waited for a title, we wouldn't be talking about him today. When he went out to face Goliath, the whole army was watching him. And what's interesting is that David wasn't

a general. He wasn't a corporal. He wasn't a
sergeant. He wasn't even enlisted. He didn't have
a title, a name badge, a uniform, or a single cre-
dential. He could have said, "I can't do anything
great. I don't have a position. I am just a shepherd. Nobody is celebrating me. Nobody is vali-
dating my gifts." In fact, it was just the opposite.
People were telling him how he was not qualified, how he was too small, how he was going to
get hurt. That didn't bother David. His attitude
was, *I don't need a title. I don't need a position. You
didn't call me, and you don't have to approve me.
God chose and called me. He gave me this gift. It
may seem small or insignificant to you, but I'm not
here to impress you. I'm not here to please you. I'm
here to fulfill my destiny.* He went out and defeated
Goliath. In a few years they gave him a title: King
of Israel. Use your gifts, and the titles will come.

"Well, Joel. As soon as they crown me King
of the Office, I'll start being my best." "As soon
as they make me the sales manager, I'll show up
early and give it my all." It works the other way

around. You have to show them what you have, then the approval, then the recognition, then the reward will come.

When my father was seventeen years old, he gave his life to Christ, the first one in the family. He knew that he was called to preach, but his family was very poor. They lost everything during the Great Depression, barely had enough food, and didn't have any money. He couldn't afford to go to college. He didn't have a position or title. No denomination was backing him up, and none of the family was saying, "John, follow your dreams. Do what's in your heart." His family told him, "John, you better stay here on the farm with us and pick cotton. You're going to get out there and fail."

Daddy could have thought, *I feel this calling. I know I have something to offer if somebody was just behind me.* But he didn't wait for a title or a position. He didn't wait for people to validate him. At seventeen, he started hitchhiking to different towns to minister in the seniors' homes, in the prisons, and on street corners. He used what he had. It didn't seem like much. Compared to other ministers who had been to seminary and had training, he would have been considered insignificant, unqualified, and inexperienced. But you can't wait for people's approval to do what God has chosen you to do.

What you have may seem small. You could feel intimidated, thinking that you don't have the qualifications, the title, the position. That's okay. Neither did David. Neither did my father. If you use what you have, God will breathe on it. His anointing on that simple gift will cause you to step into the fullness of your destiny.

We Each Have Our Own Assignment

In the Scripture, there was a little boy. All he had was a sack lunch—five loaves of bread, two fish. Nothing much. Not very significant. Yet, when thousands of people were hungry, Jesus took his lunch, multiplied it, and fed the whole crowd.

Think about this. The little boy's mother got up early that morning to make the lunch. She baked the bread and cooked the fish, then she went out and picked some fruit off the tree, dug some vegetables out of the ground. She could have been considered insignificant. She was a homemaker raising a child. Other people were out doing more exciting things, being celebrated, making a splash. If she wouldn't have been comfortable with who she was, accepting her assignment and secure in her gifts, she would have been out competing, trying to outperform others, thinking, *I'm falling behind. They're making me look bad. I'm just making a lunch. I don't have an important title.*

But titles don't bring fulfillment. Keeping up with your neighbors doesn't bring happiness. Trying to impress all your friends will make your life miserable, but running your race, understanding that God has chosen you and given you an assignment, and being comfortable with who God made you to be is what brings true fulfillment. We hear a lot about the little boy being willing to give the lunch, but it all started when his mother took time to make the lunch. She used her gift that seemed small. Just making a lunch. But God took the lunch, multiplied it, fed thousands, and we're still talking about it all these years later.

Don't discount the gift God has given you. It may seem small just making a lunch for your children, but you don't know how God is going to use the child for whom you're making the lunch. You may be raising a president, a world leader, a great scientist, an entrepreneur, a business leader, or a pastor. You may not touch the world directly, but your child may change the world. Your assignment may be to help your seed go further. Are you secure enough to play the role that God has given you? Are you comfortable enough to not have to be number one, to be in the front, to have the title, the position, to keep up with others? We put so much emphasis on rising to the top, in being the leader. And yes, I believe in excelling and having big gifts and big dreams, but I also know that everyone can't be the leader. Everyone can't run the company. Everyone can't be on the platform. Somebody must open the doors. Somebody has to play the music. Somebody has to show people where to sit and where to park. The beauty of our God is that He has given us each an assignment. Every one of us has a specific gift and purpose.

What Is Your Assignment?

Think about this. Who was more important? The little boy with the lunch or the mother who made the lunch? Without the mother, we wouldn't be talking about the miracle. Who is more important? As the senior pastor, am I more important than the ones who open the building? Without them, we couldn't get in. Or is it the ones who turned on the lights, the sound system, and the cameras? Or perhaps the ones who paid the bills during the week? Or maybe it's the ones who poured the foundation some forty years ago and built the beautiful facility? Or maybe it's the ones who have supported the ministry down through the years? Here's the point. The answer is that we're all equally important. Without one, the whole thing wouldn't function properly. Be secure enough to play your role.

We look at who's in front, getting the credit and recognition. They're the leader. A lot of times we look up to them and admire them. That's where we want to be, but if that's not where we're chosen to be, if it's not where we're gifted, if it's not a part of our assignment, then we're going to be frustrated because it's not happening. If we do get there, we'll be frustrated trying to keep ourselves there, because if you promote yourself and manipulate your way into a position, you will have to constantly work to try to stay in that position. But where God takes you, He will keep you. Where you force your way, you have to keep yourself.

It's much better to have the attitude, *I don't*

have to be ahead of my friend to feel good about myself. I don't have to be on the main stage. I'm happy being in the background. I don't have to be the little boy with the lunch. I'm happy to be the mom who made the lunch. I'm happy to sing in the choir. I'm happy to make my company look good.

When you're not competing, not comparing, not trying to be something that you're not, life gets a lot freer. It takes all the pressure off. And yes, I realize there are some positions that carry more weight and more importance, but in God's eyes the usher is just as important as the pastor. The people who clean the building are just as important as the people who own the building. The administrative assistant is just as important as the supervisor.

God is not going to judge you based on your neighbor's gift or your brother's gift or by how high you rose in the company. He is going to judge you based on the assignment that He has given you. Did you run your race? Not, did you outperform your neighbor, were you more successful than your cousin, did you get more credit or recognition than your colleague? You're not competing with them. They're running a different race.

God is going to say to Queen Esther, "Did you have the courage to step up and save the nation as I chose and gifted you to?" He is going to ask the little boy's mother, "Did you get up early and make the lunch as I gifted you to?" Two different assignments. Two different giftings. God is not going to compare. He's not going to say, "Oh, Esther. I'm prouder of you. You did so much more than the boy's mother who just made a little lunch." No, it's all going to be about whether or not we fulfilled our assignment.

Don't Be Distracted by Others

A few years ago I was out running. There was a man in front of me about a quarter of a mile who was running a little slower than me, so I decided to try to catch him. I had about a mile to go before I needed to turn off and head down my path. I picked up the pace, and I could tell every block that I was gaining on him. In a few minutes I was only about a hundred yards behind him, and I started really pushing it. You would have thought I was in the final lap of the Olympic Games. I finally caught up to him, passed by him, and felt so good that I beat him. Of course, he didn't know we were racing! The funny thing is that when I got my mind back on what I was doing, I realized I had missed my turn. I was so focused on trying to catch him that I went about six blocks out of my way. I had to turn around and go back.

That's what happens when we're competing with other people, trying to outperform them, dress better than them, make sure we're more successful. We end up competing in a race that we were never supposed to be in. Take the pressure off. It's very freeing to say, "I'm okay with you being ahead of me, getting more recognition, and doing something more exciting. I'm not going to feel bad about myself. If you have a bigger house, a badder car, and more success, you have what you need for your assignment. I have what I need for my assignment. I don't have to keep up with you. I'm not in the same race." You're not really free until you know you're not competing with anyone else.

This is one of the reasons why King Saul lost the throne. He had been happy running his race. Life was good until he heard some women saying, "Saul has killed thousands, and David has killed tens of thousands." From that moment on, he never looked at David the same way. What was his problem? He couldn't handle somebody getting ahead of him. He was fine as long as he was number one, but he couldn't handle being number two. He got distracted and spent months and months trying to kill David, all because he wasn't comfortable with who he was.

Maybe like Saul you're at the one thousand level but you have a friend who's at the ten thousand level. The real test to see if God can promote you is, can you celebrate people who pass you by? Can you be happy for them and stay focused on your race, or does it frustrate you and cause you to think, *I have to catch up with them.* Our attitude should be, *I may not be a ten-thousand-level person. God may have made me to be a one-thousand-level person, but I can promise you this: I'm going to be the best one-thousand-level person you've ever seen. I'm not going to stop at 950, 980, or 999. I'm going to become all God has created me to be.*

Don't Compare Yourself. Celebrate Yourself.

Your race is run by one person: you. Don't get distracted with competing against a neighbor, a friend, or a coworker. Just run your race. Here's a phrase I like: *Don't compare yourself. Celebrate yourself.*

Somebody else may have conquered ten thousand. You've conquered a thousand, but you know what? A thousand is still good. Celebrate what you've accomplished. Very few people today can say, "I like myself. I'm happy with my gifts. I know that God has chosen me, and I am satisfied with who He made me to be." Remember, you don't have to have a great gift for God to use it in a great way. It may seem small, like making a child's lunch or slinging a rock as David did, but when you use what you have, God will breathe on it and do amazing things.

3

You Have Favor to Fulfill
Your Purpose

What God has in your future you can't accomplish on your own. There are places He's going to take you that you can't get to by yourself. There will be obstacles that look too big, dreams that seem impossible. You're going to need assistance for where you're going. The good news is, because you have been chosen by God, He has put something on you that gives you an advantage, something that will open doors that you can't open, something that will make you stand out in the crowd. It's called "favor." Favor will cause good breaks to come to you. Favor will take you from the background to the foreground. Favor will give you preferential treatment, things you don't deserve. You weren't next in line, but you got the promotion. On paper it didn't make sense, but the loan went through. That person who was so against you—for some reason they've changed. Now they're for you. That wasn't a coincidence. That was the favor of God.

We can work hard, be faithful, be diligent, and that's important, but that will only take us to a certain level. We'll go as far as our education, as far as our background allows. But when God breathes His favor on you, things will happen that you couldn't make happen; opportunities will open that you didn't see coming. The right people will track you down. I've heard it said, "One touch of favor is worth more than a lifetime of labor." Just one good break, one phone call, meeting one person can catapult you to a new level. You've worked hard. You've been faithful. You've honored God. Now get ready for favor. Get ready for God to show out. He's about to do something unusual, something that you haven't seen, good breaks that you didn't work for, a promotion that you didn't deserve. You can't explain it. You can't take credit for it. It's the favor of God.

God chose Noah to build an ark, a 450-foot-long boat. Noah wasn't a builder. That wasn't his profession. It seemed impossible, but God will never ask you to do something and not give you the favor to do it. You have favor. The question is, do you have the faith? Are you going to talk yourself out of it? "I don't have the resources. I don't know the right people. I don't have the talent." That's okay, because you have something that makes up for all of that: Favor is on your life.

It's good to have education, but education alone is not enough. Talent alone is not enough. You need favor for where you're going. You may not know the right people, but don't worry, God does. He has already lined up divine connections, people who will come into your life and use their influence to open doors, to give you opportunity that will push you forward. You don't have to manipulate people, try to convince them to like you, or compromise to get your way. If someone is not for you, you don't need them. Don't waste time trying to win them over. The people whom God has lined up for you don't have a choice. They may not like you, but they will help you anyway. They will go out of their way to be good to you. You don't have to find them. They will find you. You keep honoring God, believing and expecting. The favor on your life will cause the right people to show up.

The people in Noah's day didn't care anything about God. They were living wildly, partying, and worshipping idols. God was so upset that He was about to destroy the Earth through a great flood. He could have wiped everyone out and started over, but the Scripture says, "Noah found favor in the eyes of the Lord." Why did he find favor and not all the other people around him who were about to perish? The next verse says, "Noah continually followed God's will and did what was right." Noah could have compromised, fit in, done what everyone else was doing, but he made the choice to walk in obedience. When you honor God, when you keep Him first place, you will find favor in the eyes of the Lord. There is a blessing on your life that will push you up when others are going down.

Favor Brings You into Prominence

"Well, if I have favor, why am I having these difficulties? Why did these people come against me? Why did business slow down?" Having favor doesn't mean you won't have challenges, but favor is what's going to keep the challenges from defeating you, and sometimes God will put you in a situation so He can show you His favor. One definition of *favor* is "to endorse, to bring to prominence, to give notoriety." If you ask someone to endorse your book, you find a person who has more influence, more credibility, a bigger following than you. When they put their name on your book, their prominence instantly gives you more credibility.

Over the years, when Oprah Winfrey has used her book club to endorse books, the authors are often unknown. Nobody has ever heard of them. Without the endorsement, the book might sell a few thousand copies. But when Oprah would say on her talk show, "This is a great book. You should read it," that simple endorsement could cause the book to sell hundreds of thousands of copies.

It's great to have people's endorsement, but you need to get ready. The Creator of the universe is about to endorse you. God is going to make things happen that are so big, so amazing, that people will know it couldn't have been just you. The medical report said you were done. "How'd you get well?" God endorsed you. His favor caused you to overcome what looked impossible.

"How'd your business become so successful? How'd you get so far ahead? We went to the same school." God endorsed you. He showed His favor so people would know that you belong to Him.

This is what happened to Daniel in the Scripture. Favor didn't keep Daniel out of trouble. The trouble was a setup for God to endorse Daniel, to bring him into prominence. Daniel was a young man living in a foreign country. The king made a decree that no one could pray to any god except to the king himself. But Daniel worshipped Jehovah. He made the decision that he wasn't going to compromise, so he kept praying just as he did every day. Some people saw him praying and ran and told the king. The king had Daniel thrown into a den of hungry lions. That should've been the end, but for some reason the lions couldn't open their mouths. I can hear one of those lions saying, "I'm hungry. I want to eat this guy, but my jaws are messed up."

Favor doesn't keep you out of the lions' den, but favor will keep the lions from harming you.

The next morning the king went to check on Daniel. When he found out Daniel was okay, he said, "From now on we're all going to worship the God of Daniel."

"Well, Joel, maybe that was a lucky break. Maybe the lions weren't hungry that day." No, when they brought Daniel out of the lions' den, the king had them throw the people who were against Daniel into the den. Before they hit the bottom of the pit, the lions tore them apart. When people saw that, they knew the Lord was on Daniel's side.

God is going to do some things that bring you into prominence, into new levels of influence and credibility. People can debate what you say, but they can't debate what they see. When they see you running the company, paying your house off, and graduating with honors, they'll know God is endorsing you. When they see you breaking the addiction, beating the cancer, coming out of the lions' den unharmed, and accomplishing dreams way over your head, they will know God's hand is on your life and He's about to bring you into greater prominence. You've been in the background long enough, serving faithfully, helping others with no recognition. Your time is coming.

David spent years in the shepherds' fields taking care of his father's sheep, and I'm sure at times he thought, *I don't have favor. I'll never do anything great. I'm stuck out here. Nobody believes in me.* The truth is, you don't have to have people believe in you. The Most High God chose you and believes in you. When David defeated Goliath, that one good break, that one endorsement, launched him into a new level of his destiny, and it made up for all those lonely years. You may feel like you're falling behind, like it's too late to accomplish a dream, like you'll never get well. What God can do for you in one moment will put you fifty years down the road. That's the power of God endorsing you.

The Seal of Approval

You've seen a seal of approval on certain products. It may be stamped on the outside of a company's box, and it can be on a little-known product. Nobody's ever heard of it. But when that big company chooses to put their stamp on it, their seal of approval, that product has notoriety and prominence, not because of what it is, but because of who endorsed it. The Creator of the universe is about to put His stamp on you. He's already chosen and approved you, but He's about to endorse you. He's about to go public. He's going to show people that you belong to Him. You're going to accomplish what you couldn't accomplish on your own. People are going to go out of their way to help you. You're going to defeat giants that are much bigger. People don't think you have a chance, but they don't know what's on you. They can't see the favor yet, but when God endorses you, when He shows out, they're not going to have any doubt that the Lord is on your side.

Joseph's brothers threw him into a pit and eventually sold him into slavery. He was falsely accused of a crime, put in prison for something he didn't do. All the odds were against him. But the Scripture says, "Joseph had favor in everything he did." One thing I've learned is that you can't keep a favored man down. You can't keep a favored woman down. You may have some obstacles, situations that are unfair. That doesn't mean you don't have favor. Challenges come to us all, but favor is why you're not going to stay down. Favor is why you're going to rise back to the top.

Joseph spent thirteen years in the background, being overlooked and mistreated. There were plenty of lonely nights. He didn't get bitter. He kept doing the right thing. One day, Pharaoh had a dream that no one could interpret, so they brought Joseph out of prison and into Pharaoh's presence. Now he was standing in front of one of the most powerful people of that day. Joseph interpreted the dream. Pharaoh was so impressed that he made Joseph the prime minister, second in command. I can imagine that meeting took no longer than an hour. Joseph walked in as an imprisoned slave. An hour later, he walked out as the prime minister.

You don't know what God can do in an hour. He can take years of heartache, years of being overlooked, years of praying, believing, not seeing any good breaks, and in one hour He not only can deliver you, not only bring a dream to pass, but He can do something that catapults you to a new level of your destiny. How can this happen? The favor on your life. When God breathes on you, doors will open supernaturally. Obstacles that look permanent will turn around. People who were against you will suddenly be for you.

Years later, Joseph's brothers—the same ones who sold him into slavery—came to the palace looking for food. There was a great famine in their country, and they had traveled to Egypt. Now Joseph, the prime minister, was in charge of the food supply. The brothers had done their best to keep him down, but God knows how to endorse you. He knows how to put you in a position of prominence.

You may feel like you're in a pit today. Don't get discouraged. We all have pit stops along the way in life. The good news is, that is not your final destination. God has an endorsement coming, and I've learned that the greater the opposition, the greater the endorsement. Much as with a bow and arrow, the more the enemy tries to pull you back, the more you're going to go forward. He thinks he's pulling you back to hinder you. He doesn't realize he's setting you up to shoot farther than you've ever imagined. When God says it's time, you're going to shoot into prominence, shoot into new levels of influence, leadership, respect, income, and credibility.

When the brothers saw Joseph and finally realized who he was, they nearly passed out. They thought they had gotten rid of him. But what they meant for harm, God used for good. God is not going to just deliver you, not going to just bring you out, He's going to endorse you. He's going to put you in a position of prominence where people can see you honored, respected, and admired.

You're Being Set Up for Endorsement

For over forty years, Lakewood Church was located in a neighborhood on the northeast side of Houston, and over time that area of the city became more industrial and a little more run-down. When I was growing up, Lakewood met in a small metal building, with metal folding chairs and a gravel parking lot. We had a portable wood building for the nurseries, and some people looked down on us because we couldn't afford much. We were second-class. We were at a disadvantage.

When I became pastor, there were certain people I saw during the week who weren't a part of Lakewood and wouldn't give me the time of day. They barely even acknowledged that I was there. But in December 2003, the Houston City Council voted for us to have the former Compaq Center as our building. We went from being in the industrial part of town with small roads, back in a neighborhood where hardly anybody could find us, to being on the second-busiest freeway in the nation in one of the most well-known, prestigious buildings in our city. That one good break catapulted us to levels of influence and respect that we couldn't have reached on our own in our whole lifetimes, and those same people who wouldn't give me the time of day started to ask me if I could save them seats. I told them, "Of course I will, right up by the flag."

What am I saying? God knows how to endorse you. He knows how to cause you to be seen in a different light. Don't be discouraged by where you are. God sees what's happening. He's keeping the records. He's going to make the wrongs right. He hears the disrespect. He hears them making fun. The Scripture says, "God heard Miriam criticizing Moses behind his back." They may not give you the time of day now, but don't worry, an endorsement is coming, not by people but by the Most High God. He's going to do things that are out of your league, things you couldn't make happen. He'll not only amaze you, but people around you are going to be amazed.

When people congratulated me for getting the Compaq Center, I thought, *If you only knew.* Yes, I prayed, and I believed, but God made things happen that I could never have made happen. The Scripture says, "God will turn the heart of a king." God turned council members who had been against us for years, and suddenly they were for us.

Right now, God is working behind the scenes in your life. He is setting you up for an endorsement, setting you up for something you've never seen—promotion, influence, relationships that will thrust you to a new level. That city council vote probably took ten minutes. The mayor brought the motion to the floor, there was a little discussion, and then they went around the table and fourteen council members voted. It's amazing what God can do in ten minutes. Those ten minutes changed the course of my life. It's amazing what God can do in an hour—Joseph meeting with Pharaoh. It's amazing what God can do overnight—Daniel protected in the lions' den.

"That Day" for You Is Coming

God has some of these destiny moments already lined up for you. You can't see them now. If He showed you, you'd think, *There's no way.* But when God endorses you, it's not like when people show you favor. When God does it, it catapults you ahead, and it's not going to take a long time. Yes, you have to be faithful. Joseph was in difficult places for thirteen years, but it only took him an hour to get out. He didn't see it coming. He woke up that morning thinking it was another ordinary day in prison. He didn't know that was his day to be endorsed. He didn't know that day was a destiny moment.

What God has for you is going to happen unexpectedly. You're doing the right thing, honoring Him. Out of the blue, someone will call and offer you the promotion. The medical report will say no more cancer, the contract will go through, or you'll bump into the person of your dreams. What would happen if we'd get up each day and say, "Father, thank You for endorsing me today. Let people see that I am Your child"?

As the Israelites were about to cross the Jordan River, God told Joshua, "Today I will begin to make you great in the eyes of all the Israelites." God was saying, "Joshua, this is your moment. Just as I chose Moses to lead My people, so I have chosen you. I'm about to endorse you. People are going to see the greatness I've put in you. You've been in the background serving Moses, being faithful, but today you're coming into the foreground." Not long after that, Joshua led the Israelites into the Promised Land.

The Scripture says, "That day God made Joshua great in the eyes of all the people." God has a "that day" for you, a time when He will make you great, when He will cause you to stand out, where you will accomplish things you never dreamed you could accomplish. You will know it, and the people around you will see the greatness in you.

Helen Major was a longtime member of Lakewood. She taught elementary school for nearly forty years, faithfully pouring her best into the children. She got one promotion after another, then became assistant principal, then principal. After a very distinguished career, she retired. A few months later a new school was opening in the school district. The school board voted unanimously to name it the Helen Major Elementary School. She never dreamed a school would be named after her, but God knows how to endorse you. He knows how to make your life significant, and it's not so we can say, "Look who we are. Look how great we've become." It's about letting

God's glory be seen through you. God wants to make you an example of His goodness, and if you will walk in humility and always give God the credit, there's no limit to how high He will take you.

Romans 8 says, "All creation is eagerly waiting for the day when God reveals who His children really are." That's talking about when we get to heaven, but even now, God is going to show people that you belong to Him. All creation is waiting for you to come into *that day*. The stage has been set. The audience is in place. You keep honoring God, and He's going to show people who you really are. He's going to bring you into a position of greater prominence.

You may be behind the scenes as I used to be when I was doing the television production at Lakewood, and there's nothing wrong with that, but God has something bigger. He's going to use you to accomplish something significant, not just be a small part. You're going to shine. You're going to stand out. People are going to see the greatness in you. It's good to celebrate others. It's good to cheer your friends on. It's good to admire those who are ahead of you, but God doesn't want you to live in a cheerleader mode, always thinking about how great others are. Can I tell you that there is greatness in you? You have talent, creativity, ability, courage, and strength. It's going to come out in a greater way, and when you come into "that day" when God endorses you, people are going to step back and say, "Wow, I didn't know that was in them. I never dreamed they would shine that brightly." God is going to show people who you really are.

Favor Is Given to Fulfill Your Purpose

There was a young Jewish girl in the Scripture named Esther. She was an orphan, having lost both her parents. She was living in exile in Persia. It didn't look as though she would ever do anything great, but one day the king was looking for a new queen. He decided to have a nationwide beauty contest where he would choose the next queen. The king sent people out looking for young ladies, and they brought Esther back and put her in the contest. Esther had never been groomed to be a queen, never had the training. She didn't come from a prominent family. They lined all the young ladies up in front of the king. They were all beautiful, all wearing the latest fashions; all had the best hairdos and makeup. I can imagine the king looked at their résumés. Some of them came from wealth and influence. Some had impressive résumés, great educations, were standouts in their field. There were plenty of obvious choices, but for some reason the king chose Esther, an orphan, a foreigner.

When God endorses you, it will cause you to stand out. His favor will cause you to be preferred. They could've chosen anyone for the contract; for some reason they chose you. They could've bought any house in the neighborhood; for some reason they liked yours best. There were plenty of students who deserved the scholarship; for some reason they picked you. God knows how to make you attractive. He knows how to make people like you. Sometimes they don't even know why. They can't put their finger on it. There's just something about you. That's God smiling down on you.

"Well, Joel, this sounds good, but I don't have the training. I don't have the experience." Neither did Esther. Favor is more powerful than your résumé. Favor will take you where you don't have the qualifications. Favor will open doors where you look up and think, *How did I get here? I was the least likely one.* Esther never dreamed of becoming a queen. That wasn't even on her radar. But when you come into "that day" when God endorses you, He will bring you into prominence that you've never imagined. He'll cause opportunity to come to you. Esther wasn't looking for that position. The position came to her. She was chosen by God for that assignment. She went from the background to the foreground. Later, Esther used her position to save the Jewish people from a plot to destroy them. I believe one reason God gave her such prominence is that He knew she would use the influence to fulfill her purpose.

Favor is not about having a bigger house, a better car, or more stuff. There's nothing wrong with that, but that's not why God is going to favor you. Favor is given to fulfill your purpose. It's to advance His kingdom. When your dreams are tied to helping others, to making the world a better place, to lifting the fallen, then you will come into some of those "that day" moments when God will shine more on you than you've ever imagined. When God can trust you, He will take you from obscurity to distinction.

Now you've worked hard, you've been faithful, you've honored God. Get ready, for the curtain is about to come up. God is about to show people who you really are. I believe and declare you are coming into a new level of prominence, a new level of influence, a new level of income. God is about to endorse you. People are going to see the greatness He put in you!

4

You Are a Masterpiece

Too many people go around feeling wrong on the inside. They don't really like who they are. They think, *If I was just a little taller, if I had a better personality, if my metabolism were a little faster...* Or, *If I just looked like her, I would feel good about myself.*

But when God created you, He went to great lengths to make you exactly as He wanted. You didn't accidentally get your personality. You didn't just happen to get your height, your looks, your skin color, or your assignment or gifts. God designed you on purpose to be the way you are.

He chose you to be the way you are. You have what you need to fulfill your destiny. If you needed to be taller, God would have made you taller. If you needed to be a different national-ity, God would have made you that way. If you needed to look like her instead of you, you would have looked like her. You have to be confident in who God made you to be and the calling He has given you.

Ephesians 2:10 says, "We are God's master-piece." That means you are not ordinary. You didn't come off an assembly line. You weren't mass-produced. You are one of a kind. Nobody in this world has your fingerprints. There will never be another you. If you're going to reach your highest potential, you have to see yourself as unique, as an original, as God's very own masterpiece.

When I was in my early twenties, I was sit-ting by myself on the beach in India watching the sunset. It was a magnificent scene. The water was so blue. As far as I could see, there were miles and miles of beach and palm trees. The sun was huge on the horizon, just about to set. As I sat there reflecting, thinking about my life, I heard God ask me something—not out loud but just an impression down inside. He said, "Joel, you think this is a beautiful picture, do you?"

I replied, "Yes, God. It's a magnificent picture."

"Well," He asked, "what do you think would be My most prized painting, My most incredible creation?"

I thought about it a moment and answered, "God, it must be this sunset. This is breathtaking."

"No, it's not this."

Earlier that year I had been in the Rocky Mountains. They were spectacular. I continued, "God, I bet it's the Rocky Mountains."

"No, not that."

I wondered out loud, "What could it be? The solar system? The Milky Way?"

He responded, "No, Joel. My most prized possession, the painting that I'm the most proud of, is you."

I thought, *Me? It couldn't be me. I'm ordinary. I'm just like everybody else.*

He said, "You don't understand. When I made the solar system, the waters, and the mountains, I was proud of that. That was great. But Joel, when I made you, I breathed My very life into you. I created you in My own image."

You Are God's Most Prized Possession

The Scripture says, "God has chosen you out of all the peoples on the face of the earth to be His people, His treasured possession." Don't go around feeling wrong about yourself. Quit wishing you were taller, or had a better personality, or looked like somebody else. You've been painted by the most incredible painter there could ever be. When God created you, He stepped back and looked and said, "That was good. Another masterpiece!" He stamped His approval on you.

On the inside of our shirts there's usually

a tag that reads, "Made in America" or some other country. Well, somewhere on you, there's a tag that states, "Made by Almighty God." So put your shoulders back and hold your head high. You are extremely valuable. When those thoughts come telling you everything that you're not, remind yourself, "I have the fingerprints of God all over me—the way I look, the way I smile, my gifts, my personality. I know I am not average. I am a masterpiece." Those are the thoughts that should be playing in our minds all day long. Not *I am slow. I am unattractive. I am just one of the seven billion people on Earth.* No, God did not make anything average. If you have breath to breathe, you are a masterpiece.

Now, people may try to make you feel average. Your own thoughts may try to convince you that you are ordinary. Life will try to push you down and steal your sense of value. That's why all through the day you have to remind yourself of who your Painter is. When you dwell on the fact that Almighty God breathed His life into you and chose you, approved you, equipped you, and empowered you, then any thoughts of low self-esteem and inferiority don't have a chance.

Years ago I was in somebody's home. They had many paintings on the walls, which weren't very impressive to me. In fact, some of them looked as if they had been painted by a child—very abstract, modern, paint thrown here and there. But later that evening, they mentioned how they had paid over a million dollars for just one of those paintings. I looked at it again and thought, *Wow! That is beautiful, isn't it?*

Come to find out, it was an original Pablo Picasso. What dawned on me that night is it's not so much what the painting looks like. It's who the painter is. The painting gets its value from its creator. In the same way, our value doesn't come because of what we look like, or what we do, or who we know. Our value comes from the fact that Almighty God is our Painter. So don't criticize what God has painted. Accept yourself.

Approve yourself. You are not an accident. You have been fearfully and wonderfully made.

I wonder what would happen if all through the day, instead of putting ourselves down, instead of dwelling on the negative, we would go around thinking, *I am a masterpiece. I am wonderfully made. I am talented. I am an original. I am chosen. I have everything that I need.* The enemy doesn't want you to feel good about yourself. He would love for you to go through life listening to the nagging voices that remind you of everything that you are not. I dare you to get up each day and say, "Good morning, you wonderful thing!" You are fearfully and wonderfully made.

How many of us are bold enough to say as David did in Psalm 139, "I am amazing. I am a masterpiece"? Those thoughts never enter into most people's minds. They're too busy putting themselves down, focusing on their flaws, comparing themselves to others who they think are better. Your Painter, your Creator, says, "You're

amazing. You're wonderful. You're a masterpiece."
Now it's up to you to get in agreement with God.
If you go around focused on your flaws, listening to what other people are saying, you can miss your destiny. The recording that should be playing in our minds all day long is, "I am valuable. I am chosen. I am a child of the Most High God."
Could it be this is what's holding you back? Your recording is negative. There are enough people in life already against you. Don't be against yourself. Change your recording. Start seeing yourself as the masterpiece God created you to be.

Realize What You Have

I read a story about a man who died in extreme poverty. At one point, he was homeless, living on the streets, and barely getting by in life. After the funeral, some of his relatives went to his run-down apartment and gathered up his belongings. He had a painting on the wall, which they sold at a garage sale. The person who bought it took the painting to the local art gallery to learn more about it. They discovered it had been painted back in the 1800s by a famous artist and was extremely valuable. It ended up selling at an auction for over three million dollars. That man lived his whole life in poverty because he didn't realize what he had.

In the same way, every one of us has been painted by the most famous Artist there could ever be. But if you don't understand your value, you go around thinking, *I'm just average. I'm not that talented. I've made a lot of mistakes in life.* If you let that negative recording play, you're just like the man with the painting—you have everything you need and you're full of potential, but you'll never tap into it. That's why every morning you need to remind yourself, "I am not average. I am not ordinary. I have the fingerprints of God all over me. I am a masterpiece."

There was an article in a medical magazine that talked about how researchers had scientifically calculated how much money the human body is worth. They added up the cost of all the enzymes, cells, tissues, organs, hormones; everything contained in the body. They concluded that an average-sized person is worth six million dollars. You've heard of "The Six Million Dollar Man." Well, you are a Six Million Dollar Person. You can put your shoulders back. You can have a spring in your step. Your Heavenly Father has invested six million dollars in you. The good news is you didn't even have to pay taxes on it!

Be Proud of Who God Made You to Be

Jesus said to love your neighbor as you love yourself. If you don't love yourself in a healthy way, you will never be able to love others in the way that you should. This is why some people don't have good relationships. If you don't get along with yourself, you'll never get along with others. We all have weaknesses, shortcomings, things that we wish were different. But God never designed us to go through life being against ourselves. The opinion you have of yourself is the most important opinion that you have. If you see yourself as less than, not talented, not valuable, you will become exactly that. You are constantly conveying what you feel on the inside. Even subconsciously, you're sending messages out. If you feel unattractive on the inside, you can be the most beautiful person in the world, but you will convey feelings of unattractiveness. That's going to push people away. The problem is inside. You carry yourself the way you see yourself.

I've seen just the opposite happen. Years ago I met a young lady who, on the surface, and I say this respectfully, wasn't necessarily attractive. She didn't have a lot of what today's culture defines as natural beauty, but I can tell you that inside she had it going on! She knew she was made in the image of Almighty God. She knew she was chosen and crowned with favor. She may have looked ordinary, but she thought extraordinary.

She carried herself like a queen and walked like she was royalty. She smiled like she was Miss America and dressed like she was headed for the runway. She may have bought her outfit at a secondhand store, but she wore it as though it was brand-new from Saks Fifth Avenue. All I could say was, "You go, girl!"

What was the difference? On the inside she saw herself as beautiful, strong, talented, and valuable. What's on the inside will eventually show up on the outside. Because she saw herself as a masterpiece, she exuded strength, beauty, and confidence.

Here's a key: People see you the way you see yourself. If you see yourself as chosen, blessed, strong, talented, and valuable, that's the way other people will see you. That's the messages you're sending out. But if you see yourself as ordinary, less-than, not talented, and not valuable, that's the way others will see you. Perhaps if you would change the opinion you have of yourself, if you would quit focusing on your flaws and everything you wish was different, if you would quit comparing yourself to somebody else who you think is better and start loving yourself in a healthy way, being proud of who God made you to be, then as you send out these different messages, it's going to bring new opportunities, new relationships, and new levels of God's favor.

This is what the Israelites did. When ten of the spies came back from the Promised Land, they saw how huge their opponents were. They said to Moses, "We were in our own sights as grasshoppers, and so we were in their sights." Notice they didn't say, "Moses, those people insulted us. They called us grasshoppers." They went in with a grasshopper mentality. They said, "We were in our own sights as grasshoppers." That's what they conveyed. Here's the principle at work: "And so we were in their sights." In other words, "They saw us the way we saw ourselves."

If you project feelings of inferiority, people will treat you as inferior. You may feel that you have a disadvantage similar to the Israelites. You don't have the size, the talent, or the education. That's all right. All that matters is Almighty God breathed His life into you. He chose you and created you as a person of destiny. He put seeds of greatness inside you. Now do your part. Start seeing yourself as the masterpiece God created you to be.

You Are Royalty

The Scripture talks about how God has chosen and made us to be kings and priests unto Him. Men, you need to start seeing yourself as a king. Women, start seeing yourself as a queen. Start carrying yourself as royalty. Not in arrogance, thinking that you're better than others, but in humility, proud of who God made you to be. You are not better than anyone else, but you are not less than anyone else, either. It doesn't matter how many degrees they have. It doesn't matter how important their family is. Understand, your

Father created the whole universe. When He breathed His life into you and sent you to planet Earth, you didn't come as ordinary. You didn't come as average. He chose you and put a crown of honor on your head. Now, start thinking as royalty, talking as royalty, walking as royalty, and acting as royalty.

Years ago I was in England attending a ceremony to honor the queen. When the queen walked in the room, you could feel the strength, the confidence, and the dignity. She had her head held high and a pleasant smile on her face. She waved at everyone as though they were her best friends. What was interesting was that there were all kinds of important people in that room. There were presidents of other nations, world-renowned entertainers, famous athletes, scientists, and some of the brightest, most talented people in the world. But, and I say this respectfully, the queen was not the most beautiful person in the room. There were other ladies who were younger and much more beautiful, but judging by the way the queen carried herself, you would have thought she was the cat's meow. She had it going on—strong, confident, secure. The queen wasn't the wealthiest, fittest, or most educated woman in the room, either. A lot of people would have been intimidated walking into that room, but not her. She walked in as though she owned the place. Why? She knows who she is. She's the queen. She comes from a long line of royalty. It's been ingrained in her thinking: *I'm not average. I'm not ordinary. I am one of a kind.*

No doubt some mornings when the queen wakes up, the same thoughts come to her mind that come to all of us. *You're not as beautiful as your sister. You're not as talented as your brother. You're not as smart as your coworker. Be intimidated. You're inferior.* The queen lets that go in one ear and out the other. She thinks, *What are you talking about? It doesn't matter how I compare to others. I'm the queen. I've got royalty in my blood. In my DNA is generations of influence, honor, and prestige.*

If you and I could ever start seeing ourselves as the kings and the queens God made us to be, we would never be intimidated again. You don't have to be the most talented to feel good about yourself. You don't have to be the most educated or the most successful. When you understand your Heavenly Father breathed His life into you, you too come from a long line of royalty. Instead of being intimidated or made to feel insecure by someone you think is more important, you can do like the queen. Just be at ease, be kind, be confident, and be friendly, knowing that you are one of a kind. Ladies, you may not be the most beautiful person, but be confident you're the queen. Men, you may not be the most successful, but stand up tall. You're the king. You are chosen and crowned not by people but by Almighty God.

But a lot of times we think, *I can't feel good about myself. I've got this addiction. I struggle with a bad temper. I've made a lot of mistakes in life. I don't feel like a masterpiece.* Here's the key: Your value is not based on your performance. You don't have to do enough good and then maybe God will approve you. God has already approved you.

Dare to Believe You Are Excellent

When Jesus was being baptized by John in the Jordan River, He hadn't started His ministry yet. He had never opened one blind eye, never raised the dead, never turned water into wine. He had not performed a single miracle. But a voice boomed out of the heavens, and God said, "This is My beloved Son in whom I am well pleased." His Father was pleased with Him because of who He was and not because of anything He had or had not done.

We tell ourselves, "If I could break this addiction, I'd feel good about myself. If I could read my Bible more, if I could bite my tongue and not argue so much, maybe I wouldn't be against myself." You have to learn to accept yourself while you're in the process of changing. We all have areas we need to improve, but we're not supposed to go around down on ourselves because we haven't arrived. When you're against yourself, it doesn't help you to do better. It makes you do worse. You may have a bad habit you know you need to overcome, but if you go around feeling guilty and condemned, thinking about all the times you've failed, the times you've blown it, that will not motivate you to go forward. You have to shake off the guilt. Shake off the condemnation. You may not be where you want to be, but you can look back and thank God you're not where you used to be. You're growing. You're making progress. Do yourself a big favor and quit listening to the accusing voices. That's the enemy trying to convince you to be against yourself. He knows if you don't like yourself, you will never become who God created you to be.

In Genesis 1, God had just created the heavens, the earth, the sea, the animals, and Adam and

Eve. When He finished, the Scripture says, "God looked over all that He had made and saw how it was excellent in every way." When God looks at you, He says, "You are excellent in every way." You may think, *Not me, I've got these bad habits, these shortcomings. I've made some mistakes in the past.* Get out of that defeated mentality. You may not be perfect, but God is not basing your value on your performance. He's looking at your heart. He is looking at the fact that you're trying. You wouldn't be reading this if you didn't have a heart to please God. Now, quit being down on yourself. Quit living condemned, and dare to believe you are excellent in every way. Our attitude should be, *Yes, I may make some mistakes. I have some flaws and weaknesses, but I am not going to live my life guilty, condemned. I know God has already approved me. I am excellent in every way. I am His masterpiece.*

If you're going to overcome your flaws and weaknesses, you have to not only stay positive toward yourself, but be bold enough to celebrate who God made you to be. Be proud of who you are. I know people who are good at celebrating others. They'll compliment their friends and brag on a cousin. "You have to see my neighbor. He's an awesome football player. You must meet my sister. She is so beautiful." And that's good. We should celebrate others, but make sure you also celebrate yourself. You are smart. You are talented. You are beautiful. There is something special about you. You can't get so caught up in celebrating others, putting them on a pedestal, to where you think, *They are so great, and I am so average. She is so beautiful, and I am so plain.*

They may have more natural beauty or more talent in some area, but God didn't leave anybody out. You have something that they don't have. You're good at something that they're not good at. And it's fine to celebrate them and say, "Wow! Look how great they are," as long as you follow it up by saying internally, "And you know what? I'm great, too. I'm smart, too. I'm talented, too."

One of a Kind

It's like this story I heard about the mayor of a small town. He was in a parade, riding in a float down Main Street with his wife next to him. While he was waving at all the different people, he spotted his wife's former boyfriend, who owned and ran the local gas station. The mayor whispered to his wife, "Aren't you glad you didn't marry him? You'd be working at a gas station."

She whispered back, "No. If I would've married him, he'd be the mayor."

You have to know who you are. God breathed His life into you. You are chosen. You have royalty in your blood. You are excellent in every way. Now put your shoulders back, hold your head high, and start carrying yourself as royalty. You are not average. You are not ordinary. You are a masterpiece. Get up every morning and remind yourself of who your Painter is. Your value doesn't come because of who you are. It comes because of

Whose you are. Remember, the most important opinion is the opinion you have of yourself. How you see yourself is how other people are going to see you. I'm asking you today to see yourself as a king. See yourself as a queen. Not arrogantly but in humility, for that is truly who you are.

Maybe you need to change the recording that's playing in your mind. If the message is, *I'm slow. I'm unattractive. I'm nothing special*, dare to say, like David, "I am amazing. I am talented. I am one of a kind. I am a masterpiece."

5

You Will Rise to New Levels

God has things in store for you that you don't see coming. It may seem as though you've reached your limits, you've gone as far as you can, but God is going to open doors you never thought would open. You didn't have the training, you weren't next in line, but somehow you were chosen for the promotion. God has unexpected favor for you. He's going to do things that you didn't deserve.

That's what happened in Genesis 48. Jacob was an old man and about to die. His son Joseph was the prime minister of Egypt, second in command under Pharaoh. Joseph was Jacob's second youngest son and his favorite. He'd given Joseph his coat of many colors and was so proud of him, but for many years Jacob thought Joseph was dead. His brothers told their father that Joseph had been torn to pieces and eaten by a wild animal when in fact they had sold him into slavery. Jacob was heartbroken and lived with all this pain.

Some twenty years later, Jacob found out that Joseph was still alive and in this position of great honor. Joseph eventually brought his father and his entire family to Egypt, gave them places to live, and took care of them. Now Jacob was 140 years old and about to pass. Joseph went in to say his good-byes and to receive the blessing from his father. He took his two sons with him, Manasseh and Ephraim. When Jacob saw the boys, he asked who they were. Joseph said, "Dad, these are my sons, your grandsons." Imagine how Jacob must have felt. He never thought he would see Joseph again. He'd already accepted that he was gone. Now God not only let him see his son, but he saw his grandsons. His heart was overjoyed.

As Jacob did, you may have given up on a dream. You think it's been too long. You've accepted that you'll never get well, never meet the right person, or never start that business. But what God put in your heart, He's not only still going to bring to pass, but it's going to turn out better than you thought. It will be not just your son, but your grandsons as well, so to speak. It's going to exceed what you're thinking.

Chosen and Adopted as Sons and Daughters

Jacob called Manasseh and Ephraim over and hugged them and kissed them. He said to Joseph, "I've chosen to adopt your two boys as my own sons. They will receive an equal share of my inheritance just as you and your brothers receive." What's interesting is that these boys were born from an Egyptian mother. Back then, the Egyptians worshipped idols. They didn't believe in Jehovah. She didn't have a heritage of faith. You might think God would say, "I'm not going to have anything to do with those boys. I'm not going to bless someone who comes from a family that doesn't worship Me." But God doesn't disqualify you because of how you were raised. You may come from a family that didn't honor God. There might be a lot of compromise and dysfunction in your past. The good news is, that doesn't have to stop you. As Jacob did with Manasseh and Ephraim, God has chosen and adopted you in spite of what you did or didn't do.

You may feel as though you've been under a generational curse because of how you were raised. God is choosing you to start a generational blessing. You're the difference maker. You can be the one to affect your family line for generations to come. It was extremely significant that these boys were adopted by Jacob. Not only did he overlook who their mother was, but they were grandsons, not sons. They should have had to wait another generation, forty years, to receive what Jacob was giving them. Normally their inheritance would have come from their father, Joseph. He would have passed down the blessing, the inheritance that was given to him. These boys were receiving something that they didn't deserve. This was showing us the character of God.

There are things that we don't deserve. We were off course, doing our own thing, but God, who is full of mercy, said, "I'm going to reach down in spite of your past, in spite of your mistakes, in spite of what your family didn't do, and I'm going to adopt you anyway." Paul wrote in Ephesians that God has chosen and adopted us into His own family. Because you've been adopted, you're going to come into blessings that you didn't earn and favor that you didn't deserve. Your past is not going to limit you. How you were raised is not going to keep God from blessing you.

As with these boys' mother, there may have been people in your family who didn't honor God, didn't make good choices. God is not holding that against you. He's saying, "I'm adopting

you anyway, and not as My grandchild, not as
My great-grandchild. I'm adopting you as My
own son, My own daughter." Joseph's sons
shouldn't have been heirs for another generation, but because of what Jacob did, they were
thrust forty years up the road. There are things
that should take you years to accomplish—years
to get out of debt, years to break an addiction,
years to set a new standard—but God is going
to do for you what Jacob did for those boys. He's
going to catapult you ahead. You're going to see
things happen faster than you thought. It should
have taken you a generation, but God's going to
do a quick work. Because you're honoring Him,
because you say, "As for me and my house, we
will serve the Lord," God is speeding things up.
What should have taken your whole life is going
to happen in a fraction of the time.

I can imagine that when Joseph's brothers
saw the two grandsons getting the same blessing
that belonged to them they didn't understand it.
They said, "Dad, that's not fair. We're sons, not

grandsons. You're giving them the same thing that you're giving us." Can I tell you that favor is not fair? It's just the goodness of God, and when God blesses you, don't be surprised if some people get jealous. Some people won't understand why God speeds things up for you, breaks down barriers for you. They'll start saying that you don't deserve it, you're not talented, you're just lucky. It's not luck. It's favor. It's God shining down on you, making things happen that you could not make happen.

Now stay on the high road. You don't have to convince people to like you. Some people can't handle your success, and if they walk away, let them walk. You don't need them. If they leave you, they're not a part of your destiny. Don't waste your valuable time with people who won't celebrate the blessing that God put on your life. Don't apologize for it. Don't try to downplay it. You didn't choose it. God chose you. He is the One who says, "I'm adopting you. I'm giving you what you don't deserve. I'm taking you to a new level." Wear your blessings well. It's the favor of God on your life.

Receive the Double Portion

After Jacob told his grandsons that he had chosen to adopt them, he called them over to give them his blessing. In the Old Testament, the blessing from the father was very significant and very revered. What the father spoke over the sons in his final days carried great weight and would affect the children for the rest of their lives. The oldest son would receive a double portion. That was the tradition. The blessing the father gave with his right hand was this double-portion blessing, so Joseph brought his firstborn son, Manasseh, and placed him at his father's right side so Jacob could easily reach out and touch him. Ephraim, the younger son, stood on his left. Joseph knelt down and put his face toward the ground, but Jacob, instead of reaching out with his right hand and touching Manasseh, crossed his arms and put his right hand on Ephraim and his left on Manasseh. Then he spoke the blessing over them.

When Joseph eventually looked up and saw
the crossed arms, he was upset. He got up in a
hurry and said, "Dad, what are you doing? You've
got it backward. Manasseh is my oldest." He
took Jacob's right hand and was going to place it
on Manasseh, but Jacob pulled it back. He said,
"I know what I'm doing. Manasseh will be great,
but Ephraim will be even greater. Multitudes of
nations will come out of him." God was showing
us that He doesn't always bless the way we expect.
Ephraim wasn't next in line. He didn't deserve
it. He wasn't born in the right position, but God
chose to bypass the tradition. He bypassed what
people thought would happen and did something
out of the ordinary. When Joseph tried to stop
his father, Jacob said, in effect, "I know Ephraim
was born second, and I know this doesn't belong
to him, but I'm crossing my arms on purpose. I'm
going to show him favor that he doesn't deserve."

This story is not so much about one family
member getting ahead of another. It's God showing us how He can take people from the back,

people who don't have the position, people who feel left out, and bring them to the front. God loves to choose people whom others say are not qualified. They don't have the talent. They don't come from the right family. They've made too many mistakes. Don't believe those lies. God is about to cross His arms. He's going to put you in a position that you didn't earn. You didn't qualify for it. You weren't next in line. God is going to make things happen that you didn't see coming.

You may think, as I once did, that where you are now is where you're always going to be. You've reached your limits. That would all be true except for one thing: God is going to cross His arms. You keep honoring God, being your best. He will open doors you never dreamed would open. He's going to promote you even though you aren't next in line. You'll think, *How did I get here? I didn't have the training, the experience, or the connections.* Here's how: God crossed His arms.

I think, *How did I end up in front of so many people?* Twenty-five years ago, I was running the television cameras and doing the production. I wasn't next in line necessarily, and I wasn't the most qualified. But God crossed His arms, and here I am. How did we get the Compaq Center? We weren't the most influential group in the bidding process. We didn't have the biggest portfolio or the most resources, but God crossed His arms. He took us from the back and put us in the front. How is my mother still alive forty-four years after being diagnosed with terminal cancer? God crossed His arms. He did what medicine could not do.

From the Back to the Front

We can all come up with excuses to settle where we are. "I don't have the training. I don't have the connections, the confidence, the talent, the size, the personality." God says, "I know all that. I created you. I know what order you were born in. I chose you." You may not be the firstborn son, so to speak. You don't feel as though you have what you need to go further. Don't worry. God's going to cross His arms. He's going to make things happen that you can't make happen.

In the Scripture, Gideon said, "God, I can't lead the people of Israel against the Midianites. I come from the poorest family. I'm the least one in my father's house." God said, "Gideon, I know you're not qualified, and I know you're not next in line, but I've chosen you and I'm going to cross My arms. I'm going to take you from the background to the foreground. I'm going to give you influence and ability that you've never had."

When Samson was being held in prison by the Philistines, he could have said, "God, I don't deserve Your goodness. You gave me supernatural strength, and I blew it. I kept giving in to temptation. Now I'm blind, bound, grinding at the mill, and it's all my own fault." God said, "Samson, I chose you to deliver Israel out of the hands of the Philistines before you were conceived. I knew every mistake you would ever make, and My mercy is bigger than anything you've done wrong. Yes, you should die defeated, feeling like a failure, but take heart. I'm going to cross My arms." God blessed Samson with supernatural strength one more time, and he defeated more enemies in his death than he did during his whole lifetime. You may have a thousand reasons why you can't accomplish your dream, why you can't get out of that problem. God is saying to you, "I'm about to cross My arms. I'm going to show you unexpected favor, unexpected promotion, unexpected healing, unexpected breakthroughs." You didn't see it coming. You aren't qualified. You weren't the next in line. It's just the goodness of God.

"Well, Joel, this is encouraging, but I don't know. I have some big problems. I have a lot coming against me." The Scripture says, "Is the arm of the Lord too short to deliver you?" Do you think that somehow God's arm can't reach you, that you're too far back, that you've made too many mistakes, missed too many opportunities, and have too big of a problem? Can I tell you that

God's arm is not too short to deliver you, to heal you, to provide for you, to free you, to vindicate you? You're going to see God do things that you didn't see coming. When He crosses His arms, things are going to fall into place. Good breaks are going to find you. Opportunity is going to chase you down.

A man I know owns a design company. He started with three small clients when his main competitor already had thousands of clients. Even though he was just a speck compared to them, some of the people at the other company were jealous of his work, and they would make disparaging remarks and try to belittle him. He didn't pay any attention to it. He kept running his race, being his best. One client led to another. He kept growing. New doors kept opening. Eventually he grew to the place where he passed up that other company. One day they called and asked if he would like to purchase them. Today he owns the company that used to be hundreds of times bigger than his. He told me, "Joel, I didn't see this coming. I never dreamed I would be this successful." Now the people who used to make fun of him no longer call him bad names. Do you know what they call him? *Boss.* What happened? God crossed His arms. You may not have the position yet, the influence, the reputation, or the confidence. You feel as though you're further back. That's okay. Just keep honoring God and you will come into this unexpected favor, this promotion that you didn't see coming.

The Decision Has Been Made

In the book of Luke, the angel said, "Mary, the Lord has decided to bless you." There are some blessings that come from being faithful and doing the right thing when it's hard. But there are times, as with Mary, as with Ephraim, when God has simply decided to choose you and bless you. You didn't do anything to earn it. In fact, there were plenty of reasons why it shouldn't have happened. Maybe you didn't make good choices or you had a family member, such as Ephraim's mother, whose background didn't honor God, but God, in His mercy, crossed His arms. He chose to be good to you. He chose to turn that problem around that you got yourself into. He chose to open that door that you never could have opened. That's God deciding to bless you.

This is what happened with my father. He was raised in a good family, but they didn't have any kind of faith. You would think that when God needed a pastor, when He needed somebody to carry out His will, He would have chosen somebody from a family of faith, but God doesn't always choose who we would choose. At seventeen years of age, my father was walking home from a nightclub at two o'clock in the morning as he'd done many times before, but this time there was something different. For some reason he looked up at the stars and began to think about God. He wondered what he would do with the rest of his life. His family was very poor. They were cotton farmers. He thought he'd have to pick cotton the rest of his life. It was all he knew how to do, but as he looked up at those stars, deep down he knew he was made for more. He didn't understand anything about God, but that night he felt something special.

When he got home, he noticed the family Bible on the coffee table. It was there as a decoration. Something told him to open it. When he did, it fell open to a painting of Jesus standing at a door and knocking. The caption read: "I stand at the door and knock. If you open it, I will come in." My father didn't understand theology, but he understood opening a door. The next day he went to church with a friend for the first time. At the end of the service, the pastor invited people to come to the front who wanted to receive Christ. My father wanted to go, but he was too nervous. He wouldn't budge. His friend turned and said, "John, if you'll go, I'll go with you." They walked down to the front together. My father gave his life to Christ, the first one in our family.

But I think, *Why my father? Why did he feel that pull? Why did he look up at the stars and begin to think about his destiny? Why did the Bible fall open to a painting he could understand? Why did that friend take an interest and walk down the aisle with him?* That was the Lord choosing to bless my father, and the Lord deciding to be good to my family. My father wasn't next in line to become a pastor. He wasn't qualified. He didn't come from the "right family." Can I tell you, none of that matters? When God decides to bless you, He'll show you favor that you didn't earn, mercy that you didn't deserve. It wasn't anything you did. It was just God crossing His arms. Where would I be if God had not decided to be good to my father? Where would my children be if God had not crossed His arms? My father not only went on to become a great pastor, found Lakewood, and touch the world, but Daddy broke the curse of poverty that he was raised in. He set a new standard for our family.

I believe that as God did for my father, as He's

done for me, God has decided to bless you. He's decided to bring your family in. He's decided to take you to new levels. Circumstances may say it's not going to happen, you're not qualified, you're not next in line. Don't worry. God has chosen you. He has unexpected favor, unexpected promotion, unexpected turnarounds. You didn't see it coming, and it may seem as though your family will never come in or you could never set a new standard. You keep honoring God, and you will come into these moments when God has decided to bless you.

Far-and-Beyond Opportunities

I saw a young man on television who was playing professional football. He had just caught the game-winning touchdown. His teammates were piling on him, the fans were cheering, everybody was shouting and going wild. Two years earlier he had been working at a grocery store stocking shelves. He had been a star player in college and was excited about playing professionally, but he wasn't drafted. He had been turned down by all the teams. They said he was too small. No one wanted him. He felt overlooked, forgotten. He knew he had what it takes, but nobody would give him a chance. One day, out of the blue, a coach he had never met called and invited him to try out for the team. He made the team and went on to become their leading receiver. When the reporter was interviewing him after the game-winning catch, this young man thanked the Lord, then he said, "Wow! I never saw this coming." He thought his days of football were over. He'd already accepted that it wasn't meant to be, then God crossed His arms. Not only was he celebrating the victory, but everyone was celebrating him.

People may rule you out; they may tell you it's never going to work out, but God has the final say. He knows how to take you from the background to the foreground. When He decides to bless you, things are going to happen that you didn't see coming. You don't have to be the most qualified, the most experienced, or from the most influential family. If you are, that's great. God can still take you higher. You may feel that you have disadvantages, and some you have no control over—what family you were born into, what nationality, what social standing. Ephraim couldn't help it that he wasn't the firstborn son. He couldn't help it that his mother had worshipped idols. He had no say over that. On the surface, that could hold you back and cause you to think, *Too bad for me. This is my lot in life*, but God doesn't choose the way we choose. He's about to show you influence, ability, and opportunities that you didn't see coming.

King David said, "Who am I, O Lord, and what is my family that You would take me this far?" He was saying, "I wasn't the biggest, strongest, or the most qualified. I didn't come from royalty. I was a shepherd working in the fields, minding my own business, and, Lord, look where You've taken me." He didn't have to go after it. It came after him. The prophet Samuel showed up at his house to anoint him as God's choice to be the next king of Israel.

God has some far-and-beyond opportunities that are about to come looking for you. The right people are going to track you down. You couldn't make it happen. It's the arm of the Lord reaching down to promote, to elevate, to increase you. You're going to look back and say, as David did, "Wow, God! I never dreamed You'd take me to this level." Now keep your faith out there. Thoughts will tell you it's never going to happen. Get ready. God's about to cross His arms and take you from the background to the foreground. You're going to step into new levels and see His favor in greater ways.

About the Author

JOEL OSTEEN is a *New York Times* bestselling author and the Senior Pastor of Lakewood Church in Houston, Texas. Millions connect daily with his inspirational messages through television, podcasts, Joel Osteen Radio on Sirius XM, the Joel Osteen Network, and global digital platforms.

We Want to Hear from You!

Each week, I close our international television broadcast by giving the audience an opportunity to make Jesus the Lord of their lives. I'd like to extend that same opportunity to you.

Are you at peace with God? A void exists in every person's heart that only God can fill. I'm not talking about joining a church or finding religion. I'm talking about finding life and peace and happiness. Would you pray with me today? Just say, "Lord Jesus, I repent of my sins. I ask You to come into my heart. I make You my Lord and Savior."

Friend, if you prayed that simple prayer, I believe you have been "born again." I encourage you to attend a good Bible-based church and keep God first place in your life. For free information on how you can grow stronger in your spiritual life, please feel free to contact us.

Victoria and I love you, and we'll be praying for you. We're believing for God's best for you, that you will see your dreams come to pass. We'd love to hear from you!

To contact us, write to:

Joel and Victoria Osteen
PO Box #4271
Houston, TX 77210

Or you can reach us online at joelosteen.com.

(f) (o) (X) @JoelOsteen

Stay encouraged *and* inspired all through the week.

Download the Joel Osteen Daily Podcast and subscribe now on YouTube to get the latest videos.

 SiriusXM   Spotify   Apple Podcasts   YouTube

Joel Osteen
NETWORK

Experience *faith and hope 24 hours a day, 7 days a week.* **All Free-to-Watch**

Streaming now on

 DIRECTV+ PLUS freevee XUMO PLAY

VIZIO The ROKU Channel